careers with the
CIRCUS

Karin Kelly

photographs by
Milton J. Blumenfeld

Lerner Publications Company

LIBRARY OF CONGRESS CATALOGING IN PUBLICATION DATA

Kelly, Karin.
Careers with the circus.

(An Early Career Book)
SUMMARY: Introduces the varied careers in a circus
including that of a ringmaster, wild animal trainer, clown,
aerialist, band leader, producer, and press agent.

1. Circus—Vocational guidance—Juvenile literature. [1. Circus—Vocational guidance] I. Blumenfeld, Milton J., illus.
II. Title.

GV1801.5.K44   791.3′023   74-11902
ISBN 0-8225-0326-3

International Standard Book Number: 0-8225-0326-3   Library of Congress Catalog Card Number: 74-11902

3   4   5   6   7   8   9   10   85   84   83   82   81   80   79   78   77

Would you like to work with the circus?

Would you like to entertain people? Would you like to work with animals or do acrobatics? Would you like to travel a lot? If you would be willing to do these things and to practice for many hours, then the circus is for you!

The circus is enjoyed by millions of adults and children every year. People love the mystery and excitement of the circus. Though the performers make their acts look easy, they are really working hard at a craft that took them years to learn. They fool us by making their difficult jobs look like fun.

Many people work together to make the circus exciting and successful. We will meet some of them in this book.

RINGMASTER

When, over the happy shouts of the crowd and the thump of the band, the ringmaster says, "Lade-e-e-z and gentlemen, . . ." an excited hush falls over the auditorium. The show is about to begin.

The ringmaster helps to make the circus exciting in many ways. Before every circus act, the ringmaster tells the audience about the history of the act. During the act, he or she points out the things that make it especially dangerous or thrilling.

Ringmasters are also responsible for helping to run the show smoothly. By blowing their whistles, they signal the beginning and end of each act to the performers and to the band.

WILD ANIMAL TRAINER

The lions and tigers that perform in the circus may look almost tame. They can balance on rolling balls, sit on their hind feet, and even jump through hoops of fire. But their roars and snarls give them away. For in their natural homes in the jungles and forests, lions and tigers are mighty hunters, strong and fierce.

The wild animal trainer works hard to teach the lions and tigers how to entertain an audience. He or she is never rough with the animals. The trainer knows that patience and gentleness work better than bullying. He or she uses a whip or a cap pistol only to signal the animals when it is their turn to perform.

CLOWN

The clown in this picture is doing what he is best known for—entertaining children. There is perhaps no other show business personality who appeals so directly to young people.

Clowns wear makeup that makes them look either very happy or very sad. They wear baggy, funny clothes and big floppy shoes. Clowns seldom speak. They make people laugh at what they do, not at what they say. For example, some clowns act very awkward—they trip and fall down hard on their behinds. All children can identify with this kind of "broad," or slapstick, humor.

Clowns must be highly skilled to do their acts. They must know how to take a pratfall without hurting themselves. Many clowns are also acrobats and jugglers.

JUGGLER

Can you throw a ball straight up into the air and catch it with one hand? Can you throw two balls into the air and catch them? Can you keep three balls moving from hand to hand at the same time? If you can do these things, you could learn to be a juggler.

Jugglers can keep many kinds of things in motion. They can juggle balls, hoops, clubs—anything that can be tossed and caught. Sometimes they balance one object on their heads while they juggle other objects with their hands. This requires real concentration. If jugglers do not pay close attention to what they are doing, they will drop the objects they are juggling.

Some jugglers do unusual things while they are working. The performer in the picture hangs by her long hair while she juggles.

DOG TRAINER

Dogs have long been good workers and companions for people. They are willing to learn almost anything a person wishes to teach them. Dogs can be baby-sitters and play-mates for children. They can guard and herd cattle and sheep; they can guide sightless people. And they are favorite performers at the circus!

The things circus dogs do are quite amazing. The dog in the picture catches balls in its mouth, one at a time, and drops them in the little nets at the side of its platform. Dog trainers work long hours to teach dogs "tricks" like this.

Dog trainers teach by repetition and reward. They repeat their commands many times until the dogs learn what to do. When the dogs do the right things, they receive rewards—tempting bits of food and lots of love.

CYCLIST

Like many circus performers, these cyclists are all members of the same family, a family that has worked with the circus for many generations. They began to learn their craft when they were very young.

This performer is riding a unicycle—a bicycle that has only one wheel. It is not easy to ride a unicycle. This cyclist learned by riding up and down beside a wall. Whenever he felt he was going to tip over, he touched the wall for support.

Circus cyclists ride many different types of cycles designed especially for them. Some are bicycles that fall into two parts. Some are very tall unicycles.

Cyclists ride in different ways, too. They sometimes stand on their shoulders on the cycle seat and pedal with their hands. That takes perfect balance.

HIGH WIRE ARTIST

Good balance is a trait that many circus performers must have. And those who need it most are the performers who walk on ropes and wires suspended high over the circus rings. Performers who walk on ropes are called tight rope walkers. Actually, a tight rope is not absolutely tight and taut. It sways a little as the performer walks on it. The high wire, however, is very taut. It is a thin wire, not a rope. Both the tight rope and the high wire demand great skill of the performers.

The high wire artist in the picture is walking the wire with baskets on her feet. She uses the long pole to help her keep balanced. This high wire artist can do somersaults on the wire and ride a bicycle across it. Like all circus performers, she does her act with grace and showmanship.

ELEPHANT TRAINER

Elephants are among the most interesting animals at the circus. In spite of their tremendous size, they can do many of the things the smaller animals can do. And because of their long trunks, they can do things the other animals can't do. Elephants can sit up with their front feet in the air; they can walk on huge rolling cylinders; they can stand and walk on their hind legs. Like the beautiful male elephant in this picture, they can also carry circus performers on their tusks, trunks, and backs.

Most elephants are trained when they are very young. By the time an elephant is six or seven years old, it can already do many of the tricks the grown-up elephants can do. Elephant trainers take very good care of their animals. They must keep them warm and give them special food to keep them healthy.

AERIALIST

There are many kinds of aerialists. These performers do acrobatics on swings high in the air. Some aerialists work in groups. They swing and somersault through the air from one swing, or flying trapeze, to another. Some work alone on a swinging trapeze. Some do handstands and headstands on a trapeze that is held still. The aerial acts are some of the most thrilling at the circus.

Many aerialists, like the young girl in this picture, begin to learn their craft when they are very young. Both the mother and father of this girl were aerialists, and they taught the girl all she knows about the trapeze. Because her family moves with the circus from place to place, she cannot go to school like most children. So she takes courses by correspondence, or through the mail.

BAREBACK RIDER

These bareback riders are a family of five: mother, father, two brothers, and a sister. Their ancestors have worked in circuses for the past seven generations. Not many of us can trace our families back so far into the past.

The mother and father trained their children. "Practice, practice, practice," the father said. And that is what they all still do, for they must learn how to do daring acrobatics on the backs of moving horses.

The riders use special horses, chosen for their large size, nice dispositions, and steady gaits, or trotting speeds. The bareback riders put a sticky substance called rosin (ROZ-in) on the horses' backs. This helps to keep their hands and feet from slipping. But even then, it is not easy to somersault from a trampoline to the back of a horse without falling down hard!

DAREDEVILS

Often, the most thrilling moments at the circus come at the very end of the show when the daredevils do their acts. Daredevils, as their name tells us, are circus performers who do especially dangerous, different, and exciting acts. In some famous daredevil acts, a person is shot out of a cannon into a net at the far end of the arena. In others, someone jumps from a very high platform into a small tank of water.

The daredevils in the picture are doing several things at once. One rides a trapeze while another steers a fast motorcycle around a narrow platform high above the ring. Motorcycles are always exciting to watch when daredevils ride them. Some jump their cycles off platforms and over many rows of cars. You should wait until you are grown up before you try to be a daredevil.

BAND LEADER

The circus band does many things for the performers and for the show as a whole. It sets the mood for an act by playing music that is jolly and happy, or rhythmic and melodious, or scary and tense. When the drummer plays a long drum roll, everyone knows that a performer is about to do a feat that is dangerous or difficult.

The circus band leader must know what kind of music to play for each act. The leader gives each performer a "cue," or signal, when his or her act is about to begin. After the act has begun, the band leader directs the music so that it follows the action of the performance exactly. When the horses canter, or when the aerialists swoop and dive, the band plays according to their rhythm.

PROPERTY SUPERINTENDENT

When the circus packs up and moves to a new city for a new engagement, there is a great deal of equipment that must be moved with it. And when it gets to the new city, the equipment must be set up in the arena where the circus will take place. The property superintendent is in charge of packing, moving, and setting up the circus equipment. Workers called "riggers" help him with this job.

The property superintendent must know exactly when and where each act is to appear in the show. He makes sure that the performers' equipment, or rigging, is put up so that their acts will be seen clearly by everyone who comes to the circus. The property superintendent is also very safety-conscious. The performers who work on high wires and trapezes depend on him for safe, strong rigging.

PRESS AGENT

People always know when the circus is coming to town. Long before the show arrives, it is advertised in newspapers and on television and radio. The ads tell people about the fabulous animals and daring performers they can expect to see at the circus. The circus press agent arranges for posters and advertisements. He or she sees to it that people become excited about the circus.

The press agent tells reporters about the specialties of each act. When an act has an especially long or interesting history, the agent tells the story to the press. In the picture, the press agent is giving a reporter a story about the circus elephants.

Press agents keep very busy at their jobs. They work all day long helping to introduce the circus to the people of the city.

PRODUCER

The circus producer puts the whole show together. He or she must know what makes the circus exciting to watch, and how to schedule each act so that it makes a real impact on the audience. The producer will often start the show with a fast-action act, like the animal trainer's, to capture everyone's attention. Then the producer will follow it with a clown act to release the tension that has built up. In a three-ring circus, the producer may schedule an exciting act in one ring to keep the audience from seeing the riggers as they change equipment in another ring.

The producer is also the administrator of the circus. He or she provides the equipment and arranges the travel schedule. The producer hires the performers and pays their salaries. A good circus producer must have many years of experience with circus life.

Circus careers described in this book

Ringmaster

Wild Animal Trainer

Clown

Juggler

Dog Trainer

Cyclist

High Wire Artist

Elephant Trainer

Aerialist

Bareback Rider

Daredevils

Band Leader

Property Superintendent

Press Agent

Producer

A letter from a circus producer

HUBERT CASTLE INTERNATIONAL 3 RING CIRCUS

A SPANGLELAND FANTASY

HUBERT CASTLE

1960 PEAVY ROAD
DALLAS, TEXAS 75228

Dear Readers,

Cooperating with the publishers of this book has been a privilege for me and the many circus performers and personnel involved. We hope that you will find <u>Careers</u> <u>with</u> <u>the</u> <u>Circus</u> interesting.

The circus is a happy, healthy way of life that offers many rewards beyond financial benefits. There is great personal satisfaction in the welcoming of each new challenge and in each achievement accomplished.

Should you consider the circus as a career, you will have unlimited opportunities for travel. And you will work with friendly people who speak many languages and who are very happy in what they are doing.

Sincerely,

Hubert Castle

The publisher would like to thank Mr. Kurt Anden and his French Poodles, Mr. Angelo Bisbini, the Cycling Wizards (the Hall family), the Diano Elephants (Lee Keener, trainer), Miss Chrys Holt, Miss Sabrina Reggittis Kaiser, Miss Malakova, Mr. Lee Marx, Mr. Gary Strong, the Trio Angelos, the Zoppe Troupe of Arabian Riders, and Mr. Hubert Castle of the Hubert Castle International Circus, for their cooperation in the preparation of this book.

The photographs in this book realistically depict existing conditions in the service or industry discussed, including the number of women and minority groups currently employed.

We specialize in publishing quality books for young people. For a complete list please write

LERNER PUBLICATIONS COMPANY
241 First Avenue North, Minneapolis, Minnesota 55401